The
GOLDEN RULES
of ACTING
that nobody ever tells you

Andy Nyman

Nick Hern Books
London
www.nickhernbooks.co.uk

A NICK HERN BOOK

The Golden Rules of Acting
first published in Great Britain in 2012
by Nick Hern Books Limited, The Glasshouse,
49a Goldhawk Road, London W12 8QP

Reprinted 2013, 2014

Designed and typeset by Nick Hern Books, London
Printed in the UK by CPI Group (UK) Ltd

A CIP catalogue record for this book is available
from the British Library

ISBN 978 1 84842 253 7

MIX
Paper from
responsible sources
FSC® C013604
www.fsc.org

Andy Nyman

Andy started his film career as Keith Whitehead in the controversial cult movie of Martin Amis's novel *Dead Babies*, which led to roles in numerous feature films including Frank Oz's hit comedy *Death at a Funeral*, cult favourites *Severance*, *Black Death*, *The Brothers Bloom*, *The Glass Man*, *Kick Ass 2*, *Automata* and *Shut Up and Shoot Me*, for which Andy won the Best Actor Award at the 2006 Cherbourg Film Festival. His many television roles include Charlie Brooker's BAFTA-nominated *Dead Set* and Channel 4's cult comedy *Campus*.

Andy's many stage roles include the European premiere of Steve Martin's *Picasso at the Lapin Agile*, the world premiere of Saul Rubinek's *Terrible Advice* and the highly acclaimed West End revival of Mike Leigh's *Abigail's Party*.

Something of a renaissance man, Andy is also a world-renowned magician and the co-creator and co-writer of the hugely popular Derren Brown phenomenon. Together they created some of the most controversial and talked-about television of a generation, including *Russian Roulette Live*, *The Heist* and *The Lottery Prediction*. Andy also co-wrote and directed Derren's stage shows *Mind Control Live*, *An Evening of Wonders*, *Enigma*, *Infamous* and *Something Wicked This Way Comes*, which won Derren and Andy the 2006 Olivier Award for Best Entertainment.

In 2010, along with Jeremy Dyson, Andy co-wrote, co-directed and starred in the hit play *Ghost Stories*. The play broke box-office records when it opened and played over 500 performances in the West End, where it terrified over a quarter of a million people. It has since been performed in Canada and Russia, and is being developed as a feature film.

www.andynyman.com   @andynyman

www.thegoldenrulesofacting.com

 @GoldenRulesBook

This book is dedicated to my family:
Sophie, Macy, Preston, Elaine, Mike, Mia,
Joe, Karen, Hugh, Louise and, of course,
Mum and Dad.

I love you all millions.

Contents

Introduction   9

Drama School   18

Auditions   24

Living the Life   36

The Business   47

Agents   58

Directors   64

Theatre   70

Filming   84

Reviews   93

Survival Tips   98

Making It Happen   112

A Final Thought   119

Introduction

This book is for anyone who has an interest in acting, from young actors aspiring to drama school, through to veterans who have spent their lives in the business. The reality is that much of this advice is 'stuff' we need to constantly remind ourselves of, myself included.

I have always loved books on acting, but while I was fascinated by actors' various methods and techniques, what I really craved was pragmatic information about what it was actually like to live and exist as a working actor. That was the material I most sought, but found most difficult to find.

This book doesn't give you any specific acting methods – there are countless books available for whatever school of acting you subscribe to. What I hope it does give you is a template of possible rules that can offer comfort and hopefully inspiration.

Every one of the rules, ideas and thoughts in this book has been learnt the hard way. I have been a professional actor since 1987, at current count that's 25 years. I have never wavered from wanting to act since the bug first bit me when I was twelve, and I honestly remain as excited about acting now as I was then. Like every freelancer, I have faced many difficult choices and challenges, but those challenges are part of what makes being 'master of your own destiny' so incredibly exciting.

Some of the advice in this book will feel brutal, possibly even bleak; it isn't meant that way, quite the opposite in fact. I believe that understanding the reality of your world is both essential and empowering. Knowledge is power, forewarned is forearmed. I have tried to be as honest as possible, so everything you'll read are my unguarded views – you may well disagree with some or many of them, but know that they have been formed through real-world experience and passed on with the best of intentions.

It's a given that as an actor you must always be creative, playful and ready to take risks, but in a flooded marketplace, I believe you must also strive to be a rock-solid professional.

Hopefully you will be able to dip into this book and leave any page ready for the next challenge facing you. I hope that these Golden Rules will save you a little pain, and keep you revved up, ready and inspired throughout your career.

This is the life you have chosen for yourself...

Ready?

"I'd rather be
a failure at
something I love
than a success at
something I hate."

George Burns

Acting in a Nutshell

Forget everything else, this is all you need to remember:

Pretend it's the first time you're **SAYING IT.**

Pretend it's the first time you're **HEARING IT.**

Pretend it's the first time you're **DOING IT.**

Drama School

If you don't get in to drama school it doesn't mean you're not good enough to be a professional actor, it just means you didn't get in to drama school.

If you don't get in, try again. Many get in on their 2nd, 3rd or 4th attempt.

Don't go to drama school because you want to be famous; go because you want to act more than anything else in the world.

Remember, the best part about drama school is that you spend all day acting. Cherish that, you may have a long wait until it happens again.

There were 25 students in my class at drama school. Only 8 of us are still involved in the business in some way.

There are many actors working in the business who didn't go to drama school.

There are currently 22 accredited drama schools in the UK – that means between 550 to 650 new actors are graduating from UK drama schools and entering the business every year.

Some teachers at drama school are terrible, some are okay and some are amazing. That's part of your training, learning who to listen to.

I was accepted at: Mountview and Guildhall (where I went). Does the fact I got into 2 drama schools mean I'm a good actor?

I wasn't accepted at: RADA, LAMDA, Central, Bristol Old Vic and Manchester Uni (where the auditioner told me I was the worst actor he had ever seen). Does the fact I didn't get into 5 drama schools mean I'm a bad actor?

Just because you get shitty casting at drama school, it doesn't mean you won't be successful as an actor.

Just because you get great casting at drama school, it doesn't mean you will be successful as an actor.

Drama school is a great big stupid joke...

...treat it like one and love every minute of it.

"I'm a skilled professional actor. Whether or not I've any talent is beside the point."

Michael Caine

Auditions

Before you enter the audition room, remind yourself: they want you to solve their casting problem, they want to give you the job. ← *Remember this.*

Be brave – make a strong decision about the character, it'll make you stand out and show that you think about your work. It'll also give the director something to direct.

For film and TV auditions, always learn the scenes you're given – it'll allow you to make eye contact with the people auditioning you and for their camera to really 'see' you.

Wear clothes that hint at the character you are auditioning for.

When working on speeches and scenes for auditions, rehearse them out loud. It will take away the fear of speaking them for the first time when auditioning.

Don't lie on your CV. It'll come back and bite you.

When you audition, you're not just auditioning for that job. You are sowing seeds for your entire career. Make the right impact and a good director or casting agent will remember you for years.

An audition is also an opportunity for you to discover what 'they' would be like to work with.

Commercial castings are a law unto themselves – leave your ego at the door and just go for it.

Treat an audition like it's a performance for a very small audience. You love acting, that's why you're an actor. Cherish the chance to act.

When auditioning for a part, if they ask 'What did you think of the script?', say something positive – otherwise why are you auditioning?

To actually get an audition is hard. Don't underestimate how many actors have tried to get into that room and couldn't. — MAKE IT COUNT.

If you get down to the final two for a job, more often than not you won't get a call to say you didn't get it – you just don't hear. It's one of the cruellest parts of the business, but it happens every day.

If you haven't worked for ages and they ask what you have been up to, tell the truth, but tell it in an unembarrassed way. 'I've been pretty quiet workwise, but I've just spent six months learning to salsa/reading plays/building my website' – or whatever you've been doing. Think about what your answer will be before you go in.

Waiting to hear back from
an audition is torture...

...it never gets easier.

Be careful of auditioning for jobs you don't want. Once you're acting in the audition room, you start to feel you could actually make something of the role and may get seduced into doing a job you never wanted. Be strong – if you don't want the job, don't go in for it.

There are a hundred reasons as to why you won't get a job – very often you're just 'not quite right'. That doesn't mean you're a bad actor.

Many actors are snobby about doing commercials, but here are three great reasons to do them:

1) It sharpens your instincts as there will be very little rehearsal time on set.

2) They are a strict discipline that teach you how to work fast and to be technical without being 'precious'.

3) You could earn a year's wages for a day's work.

Getting any job
is a miracle,
not getting a job
is the norm.

Get used to it
and don't get
downhearted.

You will not get
most jobs you
go for.

Make no mistake...

...getting a job you want is a fix like no other.

You don't have to take every audition you are offered. There will come a day when you have to say:

'No, I am bett

er than that.'

Only you can know
when that day arrives,
but when it does, it is
momentous; it is the
start of the next
chapter of your career.

A Golden Rule to live by:

Imagine

massive
success

but plan for
total
failure

Living the Life

How will you live? How will you pay your rent or mortgage? Plan on all your friends and colleagues working and you not even getting an agent. Plan for the worst – that way you will be totally prepared for both the bad times and the good.

Project, plan. Imagine where will you be 10 years from now. How about 20 years from now? What kind of work do you want to be doing? How can you help it happen? _BE PROACTIVE.

An actor's life is hard. The challenge of earning a living is hard enough, let alone the psychological challenge of staying focused and not letting your doubts and fears ruin you.

If you drink too much, smoke dope too much and party too much, you may find you have no memory left for learning lines and acting after you hit 50. That's not based on scientific evidence, just the experience of working with actors who have destroyed themselves.

You should know that if you do a play for 'profit share', 99% of the time there will be no profit to share.

Most young actors imagine being a huge star or a total failure. There is another way: most actors drift along, 'jobbing' for a living.

Pace yourself.
It's not a sprint…

…it's a marathon.

De Niro

was 30 when he made *Mean Streets*

Samuel L. Jackson

was 46 when he made *Pulp Fiction*

Kathy Bates

was 42 when she made *Misery*

Morgan Freeman

was 52 when he made *Driving Miss Daisy*

No one can know what your career outcome will be. You've got to love the journey, it's all there is.

Know who you are – don't compare yourself to anyone else. Never compare, never compete – you can only be you.

A frightening statistic – in the British Actors' Equity survey of 2010, 69% of the polled union members declared that they earned less than £3,000 a year. Read that again. Now ask yourself, how will you be in the remaining 31%?

If you're bad with money (which many actors are – myself included), when you are earning, ask your agent for advice about how to put some away for tax. They can split your payment so some goes straight into a 'tax account' – that way you can't spend it.

Get used to rescheduling your entire life. Getting a job is not only incredibly exciting, it can also be hugely inconvenient.

You have

to drop

everything.

Never forget, 'resting' is not failing, it is one of the perks of being an actor. If you wanted to work 52 weeks a year...

...you'd be
in an office.

If you are a 'jobbing actor' managing to pay your way, be proud, it's damned hard.

Do not underestimate how much stamina you need as an actor. 'Staying power' and the ability to bounce back will keep you in the game.

If you want to get married, have children, travel or climb a mountain, do it. Do not put your life on hold for a time when you are 'successful' – that time may never come, and if it does, you'll be too busy or it may be too late to do the other stuff. Live your life to the full.

You would be staggered to find out how many 'stars' spend long periods out of work, frustrated with their careers.

Old-fashioned though it may sound, your reputation is everything. Guard it, it is precious. Once it has gone you can never get it back.

You will have rough times and you will have good times, you need them both. Remember the old proverb...

"Smooth seas do not make skilful sailors."

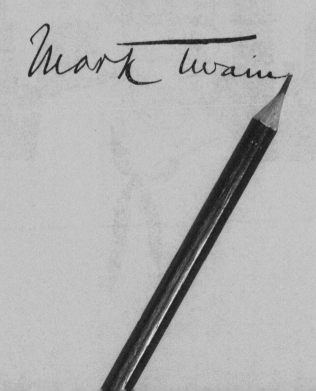

"The harder I work,
the luckier I get."

Mark Twain

The Business

What do you want? Theatre? Movies? Decide, otherwise you will coast along, aimless. Have a vision for yourself.

What would make you happy in your life and career? Really happy?

Don't ever be grateful – be proud of your work. Never accept second best from yourself.

If this is your career, your job and your livelihood, you _must_ treat it like a business. Your decisions are important, think them through.

When auditioning, rehearsing or performing, take a risk – the worst that can happen is that you get embarrassed. You won't die.

Be happy, you'll work more.

(Be warned – you're going to see this rule again.)

Don't moan. No one likes a moaner.

You will often get asked by non-actors 'How do you remember all those lines?' There is only one answer – hard work. Sadly, there is no short cut.

When it comes to line-learning, don't get swamped by the amount ahead of you, just start. Learn a few lines, then a few more. Do the same the next day, and so on. Only worry about the couple of lines you are learning, not the whole script.

Learn your lines

Learn your lines

Learn your lines

Learn your lines

Learn your lines

Learn your lines

Learn your lines

Learn your lines

Learn your lines

Learn your lines

Learn your lines

Learn your lines

Learn your lines

Oh, yes…

Learn your lines.

Ultimately, being an actor is your choice... if you don't like the life, stop doing it, no one is holding a gun to your head.

In the 25 years since I left drama school, approximately 12,500 drama school graduates have also left. Taking my year's 'drop-out' rate as average, 8,100 of those graduates will now have left the business. The life of an actor doesn't suit everyone, there is no shame in leaving if you don't like it.

You are almost powerless as an actor. The only control you have is whether you say 'Yes' or 'No' to job offers. Make that decision really count.

Do not make the first question you ask another actor 'Are you busy?' or 'Are you working?' If you do, it means you only value people if they're working. If you're resting, does that make you worthless?

You are a product, be the best product you can be.

If you are difficult or unreliable to work with, people will not want to work with you. It's as simple as that, there's no discussion on this rule.

Passion is the key to everything. If you don't have it, you will never achieve. You must adore everything.

When you get a job, work so hard that you become indispensable.

'Good enough' is never good enough – you have to work hard.

Don't just mix with actors. How can you know anything about real life if you only ever mix with people who spend their lives pretending?

Best advice ever given to me:

Keep a database or a note in your address book after every audition and every meeting. I guarantee, after 5 years in the business, you won't remember who you have or haven't met.

After each meeting fill out:

Who you met _____

The date you met _____

What job it was for _____

How it went _____

What they were like _____

Be happy, you'll work more.

(Told you you'd see it again.)

A Question
for You...

You need a new washing machine fitted in your home.

You ask a few friends for any honest workmen recommendations.

One friend suggests a plumber they used called Jack. He fitted the washing machine well, but turned up a bit late, was on the phone a lot, took a few tea breaks and left a bit of a mess.

Another friend recommends Phil. He also fitted the machine well, but he was on time, worked efficiently and made sure everything was clean when he left.

Both plumbers are available and are exactly the same price.

Which one would you call to do your job, Jack or Phil?

Now, here's the question: if that level of care and professionalism is true for hiring a plumber, why should it be any different when hiring an actor?

"To be successful in show business, all a guy needs is about 50 really lucky breaks."

Walter Matthau

Agents

Don't moan about your agent. Lots of actors do and it's tedious and ridiculous. If you're not happy with your agent, talk to them or leave them, otherwise shut up. Be different, stick up for your agent.

Despite what many actors say, your agent doesn't work for you. You are a team, work hard at making it work.

Tell your agent the sort of work you want to do, otherwise how are they expected to know?

If you have been offered a job that you really want to do, make sure your agent knows. It's essential they do not lose the job for you by negotiating too hard.

When you're waiting to hear from a job, try not to call your agent to ask if there's any news. If there is... you'll know.

Get used to hearing your agent say:

'It won't be going any further on that one.'

(You didn't get the job.)

'They're going a different direction with that role.'

(You didn't get the job.)

'They really liked you, but…'

(You didn't get the job.)

'It's very quiet at the moment.'

(There are no jobs for you not to get.)

However, here's a sentence that you will never hear your agent say:

'You got the job and they've called to say that they have a massive budget and they can pay you much more than you hoped for.'

"I deny that I said actors are cattle. What I said was actors should be treated like cattle."

Alfred Hitchcock

Directors

Some directors are brilliant at directing actors, some are okay and some are simply abysmal. It took me a while to realise that.

Trust yourself – your instincts are your best friend. You will DIY more often than you imagine.

It is always easier to try what your director asks you to do than to spend 30 minutes of precious rehearsal time discussing or arguing about it. *SO TRUE!*

There is directing and there is bullying – never be bullied, no job is worth it.

There is no feeling as exciting as finding yourself acting in a totally new way because you trusted a director's note.

Be aware... if you do short films and fringe theatre, those directors will rarely use you if they get successful. That doesn't mean don't do those jobs, but be aware of the reality of the situation.

Throw yourself into everything the director asks you to do – it's the only way you'll find out if it works or not. You may be surprised by what you learn.

If you take a
job, commit
to it, give it
everything
you have...

...Even if the job is terrible you can still excel.

"The show may start at 8pm, but for me, the curtain goes up when I'm having my cornflakes."

Anthony Newley

Theatre

During the run of a play, spend time in the day running any big speeches you have. That way, the first time you'll be saying it isn't in front of the audience. It reminds you that you know it and will boost your confidence.

Technical rehearsals are always slow, soul-destroying and miserable. Keep your sense of humour.

Always be nice to the stage crew. They work unbelievably hard and are mostly unthanked for it.

If a moment that used to get laughs, stops getting laughs, do not try harder to get the laughs back. Do less and go back to playing the truth behind the moment.

THEATRE STAGE DOOR

Theatre is unbelievably exciting. Everything from the stage door, to the dressing room, to the smell of backstage, to standing on stage actually performing. You must learn to love it all. If you don't love it... leave now.

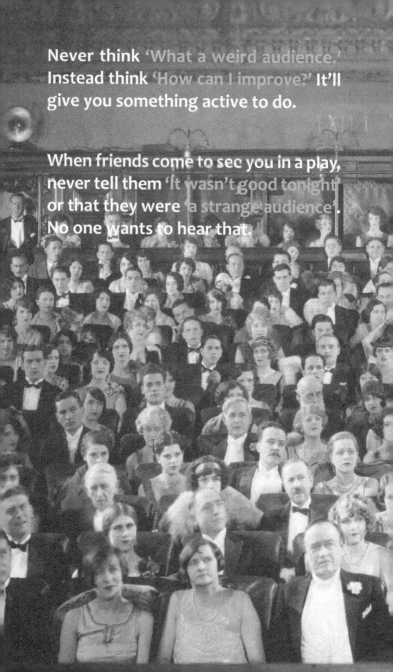

Never think 'What a weird audience.'
Instead think 'How can I improve?' It'll
give you something active to do.

When friends come to see you in a play,
never tell them 'It wasn't good tonight'
or that they were 'a strange audience'.
No one wants to hear that.

It doesn't matter if there are far fewer people in the audience than you were hoping for, you still have to give 100%. Don't worry about the audience, just tell your story.

Your job in rehearsals

is to forget about embarrassment and try every idea, no matter how odd, until you discover what feels 'right'.

Your job in performance

is to do what you discovered in rehearsal. Keep it the same every show whilst making it utterly new, fresh and exciting. It's hard, challenging work and requires great mental and physical energy.

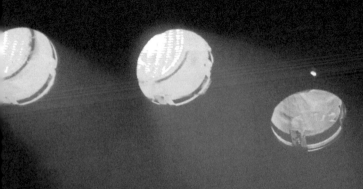

The following, allegedly true story, perfectly illustrates the 'odd lie' that theatre is.

During a note session after a dress rehearsal of *Henry V* at the Royal Shakespeare Company, the director gave the following speech to the company about the performance the battle-weary soldiers had just given:

'For God's sake, these soldiers have been in a war and are about to go back in. They started as 300 men and are now down to about 50. They have seen their comrades butchered and have witnessed terrible sights that they will never forget. I need to see that in the way you all stand, look, breathe and behave. I need this to feel as brutal and true as anything you have ever done. Also, I need you all to cheat left a bit to make sure you're in the light.'

When a director asks you to try something new, always try it at least 3 times:

The first time –
will feel terrible.

The second time –
will feel less terrible.

The third time –
will allow you to judge it properly.

DON'T BE TOO QUICK TO DISMISS!

After a rehearsal or a run when the director is giving notes to the whole cast, just take your notes – do not get into lengthy debates about what you're trying to do with your character, just take the note already!

When a director gives you a note, write it down or you will forget it.

When working in a show, take care of yourself. Be careful of your voice and always stock up with vitamins.

When working, you will make great friendships that feel like they will last for ever, but sometimes they actually only last for the duration of the job.

It's one of the sad, wonderful things about working as an actor.

"I like the ephemeral thing about theatre. Every performance is like a ghost – it's there and then it's gone."

Maggie Smith

Filming in
4 words:

'Hurry up and wait.'

Filming

'*Gandhi* in the morning, *EastEnders* in the afternoon.' A saying on movie sets that perfectly describes the way film shoots work. The morning is leisurely as though you're making art, the afternoon chaos as the time runs out.

You will spend hours and hours waiting around. Don't ever moan, **it's a brilliant adventure** – enjoy it, you'll be out of work again soon.

Try to learn the names of everyone working with you, not just the other actors.

Keep the crew list and contact sheet you are given when filming. They are an invaluable way of knowing who you worked with and how to get in touch with them.

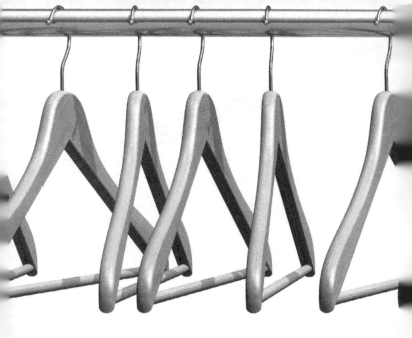

Be nice to make-up and wardrobe. They can make you look great or awful.

Don't get involved in the gossip in the make-up van – it will only get you into trouble. RESIST THE URGE!

When you wrap on a day's filming…

… always hang your costume up.

Be aware that the other departments have to keep working after you have gone home. They are not your slaves.

When filming on location, you will be given 'per diem' – this is daily money, on top of your fee, for meals and living. Spend it wisely, it is precious 'free money' and can really come in handy after the job has finished.

If you're going to a cast and crew screening of a film you are in, it can be anywhere from 8 months to 18 months since you filmed. Have a look at the contact sheet before you go to refresh your memory on people's names. You'll be amazed how many you have forgotten.

Whatever you film is there for ever. Try to be proud of every frame you shoot.

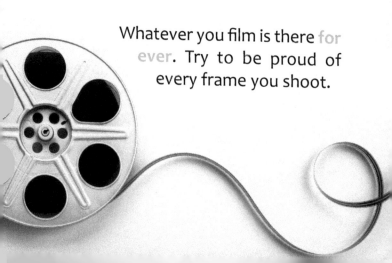

When filming, you will discover that other cast members are getting paid more than you, have nicer hotel rooms than you, are flying a better class than you, have a better trailer than you, etc., etc., etc. It's all a distraction. You are there to act – get that right and forget the rest.

"Art, especially the stage, is an area where it is impossible to walk without stumbling. There are in store for you many unsuccessful days and whole unsuccessful seasons, there will be great misunderstandings and deep disappointments… you must be prepared for all this, accept it and nevertheless, stubbornly, fanatically follow your own way."

Anton Chekhov

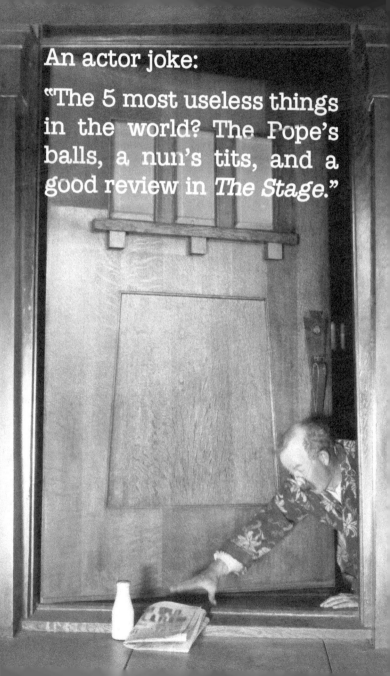

An actor joke:

"The 5 most useless things in the world? The Pope's balls, a nun's tits, and a good review in *The Stage*."

Reviews

The good ones and the bad ones will both kill you. The only difference is the good ones are sweet-tasting poison.

If you search for your name on the internet, you are asking for trouble. Every 12-year-old in the world is a critic. I call it 'The Coward's Playground'.

No one sets out to give a bad performance or to make bad work – <u>be kind</u> when talking about others.

Never offer another actor an opinion of their show or performance unless they ask for it. Even then...

When you're working, everyone's got an opinion about your play/film/TV/performance and are more than happy to tell you it. Choose the ones you listen to very carefully and ignore all the others.

Don't expect everyone to respect your opinion – even though you know you're right.

Great reviews can damage your performance as much as bad ones, especially if they refer to a particular 'moment' of yours they loved – it can kill it for you.

Many actors avoid reading reviews, and it's by far the most sensible option. I have never quite found the strength required... I wish I could.

"Let everybody shine, because that's the best way to look good."

Carol Burnett

Survival Tips

Be nice to work with – the first thing an interested employer will do is look at your CV, call someone who has worked with you and ask, 'What's he/she like?'

Actors are not 'special people'. You are no more important than anyone else at the theatre or on set. It may sound obvious, but it's staggering how many actors behave like they are above everyone else.

Whenever you book a holiday, you are guaranteed to get a job that clashes with it. Want a job? Book a holiday.

Whenever you get two jobs that clash – try to do the best role over the one that pays best.

Never harmonise when singing 'Happy Birthday'...

...this has nothing to do with work, it's just all actors do it and it's bloody annoying.

In the UK, if you do musicals, it will restrict the way casting agents see you. You will find it much harder to get seen for TV and film work.

You can always act faster than you think you can. Prove it, do a 'speed run' of a scene or speech and see if it isn't better.

'It's not what you know, it's who you know.' This is a myth, do not believe it, do not use it as an excuse for not succeeding. Nepotism may get you one chance, but a career is not built on networking and schmoozing – it is built on one thing... how good you are at your job.

No one has ever 'had it easy' or been 'really lucky'. I guarantee every actor you see has had to work hard and make sacrifices. Some people may think you're lucky and have had it easy – have you?

Don't say 'I'm nervous', say 'I'm excited.' Try it, you'll be amazed how effectively it gets rid of your nerves.

Almost every role in every play, film, TV show or commercial that you see, has involved actors auditioning for it, waiting to hear and mostly not getting it. The actor you are looking at got the call to say, 'You got it.'

No matter how bad a job is, there is always something good to enjoy. Search for it, find it and spread it. Remember, feeling good is infectious.

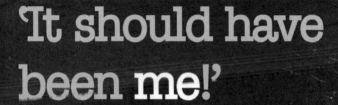

'It should have been me!'

Never get bitter and hate other people for the jobs you didn't get.

It's poison to think like that and it will destroy you.

Everybody hates read-throughs. Most actors in the room will be looking around thinking that they are the worst actor in the room.

WARNING – if you're not thinking you're the worst actor in the room at a read-through... it might be you!

Watching yourself in a film or on TV is horrible – you will think your voice sounds horrible and you look awful. Trust me, it doesn't and you don't.

Do not spend the last third of an acting job worrying about where the next job is coming from or what auditions the rest of the cast are getting. Savour every moment of every job, you don't know how long it will be until the next one comes along.

Be happy, you'll work more.

(I know, I know, that makes it 3 times, but this is so important you need to read it again.)

When are we going to see you on *EastEnders*?

Have I seen you in anything?

Are you resting?

Learn to be gracious in replying to all of these...

...good luck with that!

This may be the most important tip in the book.

This isn't just about acting, it's about life.

"Don't wear a frown,
Try positive thinking,
Laugh at your troubles instead."

Morecambe and Wise

Teach yourself to enjoy
and replay positive
memories, especially just
before going to sleep.
They will make you feel
good and it makes more
sense than replaying bad
ones, which just make you
feel miserable.

"Everything comes
to he who hustles
while he waits."

Thomas Edison

Making It Happen

Get a website.

(Don't scrimp on this, it is an important expense.)

Get a showreel.

(Don't scrimp on this, it is an important expense.)

Want to do voice-overs? Don't just talk about it.

Get a voicereel.

(And guess what: don't scrimp on this, it is an important expense.)

If you take non-acting jobs when you are resting you will:

- Earn money
- Meet new people
- Have experiences that you never imagined
- Learn more about life

You have no idea where it will lead you – there is no downside.

Develop a 'Screw You' Fund

If you can earn money from somewhere else, it means you can say 'screw you' to acting work you don't want to do. This is power and it will free you up artistically.

These are just some of the jobs I've done whilst resting:

- £ Shop work
- $ Box office
- £ Backstage work
- $ Telesales
- £ Lorry driver
- $ Van driver
- £ Shop promotions
- $ Drama teacher
- £ Conference demonstrator
- $ Kids' party entertainer
- £ Close-up magician
- $ Mentalist

There is no shame in resting, but there is shame in being lazy. Pay your way, you'll feel stronger.

If you develop a second skill or income stream, you will double your survival chances as an actor.

└ FIND SOMETHING...

We live in an age where technology has made anything possible. You can publish a book online for next to nothing, record an album on your computer, shoot and edit a broadcast-quality HD movie on your phone. You are a creative person, apply yourself and create something, anything. No excuses, just 'do'.

I can promise you this: the highs are high and the lows are low, but who wants a life half-lived?

Every audition and every job you do is an opportunity to do great work, build your reputation and therefore improve your chances of working more.

Never waste that opportunity.

A Final Thought...

Never forget why you are lucky...

You have a dream.

You have a
passion.

You are
taking a risk.

Most people
don't.

Never forget
that.

P.S.

Be
HAPPY

you'll
work
more.

TODAY

AM

PM WRITE YOUR
OWN
GOLDEN RULES.

If you have a Golden Rule you'd like to share, visit:

www.thegoldenrulesofacting.com

With huge thanks to Jeremy Dyson, Neil Patrick Harris, Matthew Macfadyen, Andrew O'Connor, Simon Pegg, Joe Sikora, Cristian Solimeno, Simon Trewin, Jemima Williams, Richard Wiseman, and Matt Applewhite, Jodi Gray and Nick Hern at NHB.

Illustrations by Jemima Williams (www.jemimawilliams.com)

Picture credits: all photographs are used under licence from Shutterstock.com **12/13** © Nils Z **18** © Kletr **21** © Francesco81 **26** © Martin Fischer **28, 42/43, 72/73, 82, 92** © Everett Collection **34/35** © Peter Cox **46** © wanchai **52/53** © musicman **54** © Andrey Burmakin **58/59** © IKO **60/61** © joingate **65** © siraphat **71** © Lance Bellers **76/77** © Lars Christensen **78, 93** © Aleksandr Bryliaev **84/85** © sculpies **86/87** © Oleksiy Mark **88, 110/111** © Jim Barber **94** © LesPalenik **99** © konstantynov, U.P.images_vector **102/103** © Bombaert Patrick **105** © Picsfive **106/107** © Stephen Coburn, aleksm **114** © olavs, Yuriy Boyko **120** © João Seabra **121** © Peter Zurek **126/127** © Robbi except **49** © Matthew Davies. Any inadvertent omissions can be rectified in future editions.